DEADLY FORCE
CONSTITUTIONAL STANDARDS, FEDERAL POLICY GUIDELINES, AND OFFICER SURVIVAL

By
John Michael Callahan, Jr.
Supervisory Special Agent
Chief Division Counsel
Federal Bureau of Investigation
Boston Division (Retired)
February, 2001

D1598118

LOOSELEAF LAW
PUBLICATIONS, INC.
Flushing, New York

Library of Congress Cataloging-in-Publication Data

Callahan, John M. (John Michael), 1943-
    Deadly force : constitutional standards, federal policy guidelines, and officer survival / by John Michael Callahan, Jr.
        p. cm.
Includes index.
  ISBN 1-889031-49-6 (pbk. : alk. paper)
  1. Police shootings--United States. 2. Violence (Law)--United States. I. Title.
    KF5399 .C35 2001
    344.73'0523--dc21   2001002225

Printed in the United States of America

1 2 3 4 5 6 7 8 9 10

TABLE OF CONTENTS

INTRODUCTION

Statistics establish that the law enforcement profession in America is an inherently dangerous occupation. Between 1985 and 1994, 708 officers were feloniously killed.[1] Over 650 of these officers were killed with firearms.[2] In 1994, 64,912 line-of-duty assaults were committed against police officers that resulted in over 23,000 officers being personally injured.[3]

These figures disclose that officers frequently are required to confront armed and dangerous subjects who are willing to violently resist arrest and to injure and kill those sworn to protect innocent citizens from harm. The need for officers to be able to lawfully defend themselves and the public through the use of force and deadly force is obvious.

This book will examine the decisions of the United States Supreme Court and the lower federal appellate courts which pertain to the use of force and deadly force by federal, state and local law enforcement officers. This examination will include a review and analysis of the constitutional standards created by the Supreme Court regarding police use of force and deadly force. Lower federal appellate decisions which have interpreted and applied these standards will also be reviewed. All of

---

1   Uniform Crime Reports, Federal Bureau of Investigation, Law Enforcement Officers Killed and Assaulted, 1994, page 15.

2   Id.

3   Id.

i

these cases are directly relevant to state and local police officers. In each case, state or local officers were the defendants. The new United States Department of Justice (DOJ) policy regarding the use of deadly force by law enforcement officers working for DOJ component agencies will also be discussed and analyzed. A practical analysis of the "objectively reasonable" police officer will also be undertaken. The focus of this objective reasonableness analysis will be upon officer survival in deadly confrontations.

CONSTITUTIONAL STANDARDS - DEADLY FORCE

The first and only decision of the United States Supreme Court dealing directly with the use of deadly force by law enforcement officers is *Tennessee v. Garner.*[4] In *Garner*, a police officer shot and killed an unarmed burglary suspect as he was attempting to flee from the scene of the crime. The officer was later sued in the United States District Court for alleged violations of the suspect's constitutional rights. The District Court ruled in favor of the officer because he acted pursuant to the state "fleeing felon" statute. The District Court determined that the statute authorized the shooting and found it to be constitutional.

The United States Court of Appeals reversed and the Supreme Court affirmed. Initially the Supreme Court ruled that apprehension by means of deadly force is a seizure subject to the reasonableness requirement of the Fourth Amendment. Next, the Court determined that the state "fleeing felon" statute was unconstitutional to the extent that it authorized the use of deadly force against unarmed non-dangerous fleeing suspects.

The Court ruled that deadly force would be appropriate to prevent escape of a fleeing felon under three conditions. First, deadly force must be necessary to prevent escape. Second, the officer must have probable cause to believe that the suspect poses a significant

---

4   471 U.S. 1 (1985).

threat of death or serious physical harm to the officer or others. Third, the officer must warn the suspect of an intention to use deadly force, if feasible.

The Court's requirement that deadly force be used only when necessary, can be characterized as its necessity component. The warning requirement can be viewed as a sub category of the necessity component because to the extent that a dangerous suspect submits to arrest after a warning, deadly force is not necessary.

The requirement that the suspect pose a significant threat of death or serious bodily harm can be labeled as the Court's dangerousness component. This can also be viewed as a sub category of the necessity component because unless a suspect is dangerous, it is not necessary to use deadly force. Referring to this component, the Court explained that deadly force may be used if necessary to prevent escape, "[I]f the suspect threatens the officer with a weapon **or** there is probable cause to believe that he has committed a crime involving the infliction or threatened infliction of serious physical harm...."[5] The Court's use of the disjunctive "or" suggests that it intended two kinds of suspects who could independently meet the "dangerousness" component. First, this component includes those suspects who threaten an officer or others with a weapon. Second, it includes those who have committed a crime involving the infliction or threatened infliction of serious bodily harm. This second category of suspect appears to meet the

---

5   Id. at 11 (emphasis added).

dangerousness component of *Garner* because of the violent or potentially violent nature of the crime committed regardless of whether they are believed to be armed at the time police are trying to capture them.

The most recent decision of the United States Supreme Court regarding police use of force is *Graham v. Connor.*[6] *Graham* involved allegations against police officers regarding the use of excessive force rather than deadly force. Nonetheless, the Court ruled that, "all claims that law enforcement officers have used excessive force – deadly or not – in the course of an arrest, investigatory stop, or other 'seizure' ... should be analyzed under the Fourth Amendment and its 'reasonableness' standard rather than under a 'substantive due process' approach."[7] The Court rejected the "due process" standard that would have required alleged victims to prove malice on the part of offending officers. The Court observed that in deciding whether an officer's conduct meets the Fourth Amendment reasonableness standard, lower courts should examine such factors as the severity of the suspect's crime, the immediacy of the threat to the safety of the officers or others and, whether the suspect is actively resisting arrest or attempting flight. The Court stated that, "The 'reasonableness' of a particular use of force must be judged from the perspective of a reasonable officer **on the scene**, rather than with the 20/20 vision of hindsight."[8] The Court explained that,

---

6   490 U.S. 386 (1989).

7   Id. at 395.

8   Id. At 396 (emphasis added).

"The calculus of reasonableness must embody allowance for the fact that police officers are often forced to make split-second judgements – in circumstances that are tense, uncertain, and rapidly evolving – about the amount of force that is necessary in a particular situation."[9] The Court also stated that, "With respect to a claim of excessive force, the same standard of reasonableness **at the moment** applies ..."[10]

The Court's analysis suggests that lower courts should examine excessive force claims with caution and remember that an officer's decision to use deadly force is often made in a split second under extremely dangerous, difficult and rapidly evolving circumstances. Moreover, the Court's use of the phrases "on the scene", "split second judgements", and "at the moment" when referring to the reasonableness inquiry, indicates that it intended that lower courts focus primarily upon the degree of danger to the officer and others "at the moment" when deadly force was used. Following such an approach would preclude endless judicial second-guessing of an officer's actions and decisions that lead up to but are separated from the decision to use deadly force.

---

9   Id.

10   Id. (emphasis added).

THE SEIZURE ISSUE AND THE OBJECTIVE REASONABLENESS STANDARD

The Supreme Court in *Garner* ruled that a Fourth Amendment seizure occurs when an officer apprehends a person by using deadly force. Likewise, in *Brower v. County of Inyo*,[11] the Supreme Court ruled that a seizure occurs **only** when there is a governmental termination of freedom of movement through means intentionally applied by the police. In *County of Inyo*, the means intentionally applied involved a police roadblock that Brower crashed into during a car chase. In *California v. Hodari D.*,[12] the Supreme Court ruled that no seizure of a fleeing drug suspect occurred until police officers were able to physically bring him under control or until the suspect yielded to a display of authority. Some federal appellate courts have used these decisions to exclude from the reasonableness analysis in deadly force cases, events leading up to but occurring prior to the suspects's actual seizure. For example, in *Carter v. Buscher*,[13] the Seventh Circuit Court of Appeals rejected plaintiff's claim that a faulty arrest plan devised by police officers created the circumstances leading to an unreasonable use of deadly force. In *Carter*, the suspect killed one officer and seriously wounded another before being killed by a third. The court ruled that no Fourth Amendment seizure

---

11   489 U.S. 593 (1989).

12   499 U.S. 621 (1991).

13   972 F.2d 1328, 1333 (7th Cir. 1992).

occurred until the suspect was shot and with respect to the reasonableness inquiry, refused to consider the soundness of the arrest plan which preceded the immediate events occurring at the time of the shootout. The court explained, "Even if the defendants concocted a dubious scheme to bring about Ruhl's arrest, it is the arrest itself and not the scheme that must be scrutinized for reasonableness under the Fourth Amendment."[14]

The First Circuit Court of Appeals rejected this line of reasoning in *St. Hilaire v. City of Laconia, et al.*[15] In *St. Hilaire*, an officer shot and killed a drug suspect who reached for a firearm during a police attempt to execute a search warrant. Plaintiff alleged that the officer failed to identify himself and the District Court declared the issue irrelevant because even if true, it occurred before a Fourth Amendment seizure took place. The District Court dismissed the suit and the Court of Appeals affirmed but rejected the District Court's rationale. The Court of Appeals ruled that once a seizure occurs, the Fourth Amendment reasonableness inquiry may include an examination of all relevant events leading up to the seizure.

At first glance, the First Circuit appears to be correct in its analysis because in assessing the reasonableness of a search, the Supreme Court has often applied a "totality of circumstances" test.[16] However, when applied

---

14   Id. at 1333. See also, *Cole v. Bone*, 993 F.2d 1328 (8th Cir. 1993).

15   71 F.3d 20 (1st Cir. 1995).

16   See, e.g., *Illinois v. Gates*, 459 U.S. 1028 (1983).

to deadly force cases, the analysis is flawed because it ignores the plain language of the Supreme Court in *Graham* which instructs the lower courts to examine the objective reasonableness of police use of deadly force "at the moment" force is used by police officers. The Court in *Graham* also explained that such cases must be analyzed from the perspective of the officer "on the scene" who is faced with making "split-second judgements" in tense, dangerous and quickly changing circumstances. If an officer or another person is faced with imminent death or serious bodily harm, the officer's failure to craft the best arrest plan or to do something else deemed prudent in retrospect, should be irrelevant to the analysis of whether deadly force was reasonable. Most federal appellate courts agree that events which occur prior to the actual use of deadly force by police officers are irrelevant to the determination of whether the officers acted with objective reasonableness.[17]

For example, in *Schulz v. Long*,[18] an officer shot and killed a person who attacked him with a hatchet. Plaintiff appealed an adverse lower court decision and argued that actions by the police leading up to the violent encounter created the need to use deadly force. Plaintiff alleged that before attempting to seize Schulz, the officers should have waited for a supervisor and called for a Special Weapons and Tactics (SWAT) team.

---

17 *Salin v. Proulx*, 93 F.3d 86 (2nd Cir. 1996);
    Greenidge v. Ruffin, 927 F.2d 789 (4th Cir. 1991);
    Drewitt v. Pratt, 999 F.2d 774, 780 (4th Cir. 1993);
    Elliot v. Leavitt, 99 F.3d 640 (4th Cir. 1996);
    Fraire v. City of Arlington, 957 F.2d 1268 (5th Cir. 1992).

18 44 F.3d 643 (8th Cir. 1995).

8

The Eighth Circuit Court of Appeals rejected this contention and stated that the Supreme Court's use in *Graham* of phrases "at the moment" and "split-second judgement" are strong indicia that the reasonableness inquiry extends to the events known to the officer at the precise moment the officers effectuate the seizure.

Likewise, in *Plakas v. Drinski*,[19] the Seventh Circuit Court of Appeals rejected plaintiff's arguments that events leading up to the shooting of Plakas should be examined to determine whether the shooting met the reasonableness standard of *Graham*. Plakas attacked officers with a raised fireplace poker and an officer shot and killed him. The court ruled that the reasonableness of the use of force must be judged from the point in time when Plakas raised the poker and charged the officer. The court explained, "We do not return to the prior segments of the event and, in light of hindsight, reconsider whether the prior police decisions were correct. Reconsideration will nearly always reveal that something different could have been done if the officer knew the future before it occurred."[20]

The First Circuit Court of Appeals has not been persuaded by the decisions of other federal circuits on this issue. Much to the contrary, the court's recent decision in *Napier v. Town of Windham, et al.*,[21] reinforces its decision in *St. Hilaire* that it is appropriate to consider

---

19   19 F.3d 1143 (7th Cir. 1994).

20   Id. at 1150.

21   187 F.3d 177 (1st Cir. 1999).

police actions leading up to a use of deadly force and examine them for their reasonableness. In *Napier*, a police officer shot and wounded a man who threatened the officer and another officer with a handgun. The court ruled in favor of the police but did consider Napier's claim that the police acted incorrectly by allegedly sneaking around his house with drawn guns rather than telephoning him or contacting him from a position of cover. Napier claimed that the police conduct created the situation which led to the shooting. The court rejected Napier's claim that such alleged conduct was unreasonable. Nevertheless, the fact that the court considered the claim, demonstrates its continued willingness to review pre-shooting police conduct for its reasonableness.

THE DANGEROUSNESS COMPONENT

In *Garner*, the Supreme Court made clear that deadly force could be used by police only when there was probable cause to believe that a fleeing felon was dangerous. The court explained that deadly force was appropriate if the suspect threatened the officer with a weapon **or** had committed a crime involving the infliction or threatened infliction of serious bodily harm or death. As discussed earlier, the Court's use of the disjunctive word "or" suggests that it intended that there be two distinct categories of dangerous persons, those who directly threaten police officers or others with weapons and those who have committed crimes involving the actual or threatened infliction of serious bodily harm or death.

Dangerousness - Threats with Weapons

A review of the federal appellate cases following the Supreme Court decisions in *Garner* and *Graham* reflects numerous cases in which police officers used deadly force in the face of direct threats to their own lives or the lives of others. Police officers have been attacked with knives[22], a fireplace poker[23], guns[24], and motor vehicles.[25]

---

22 *Roy v. Inhabitants Of The City of Lewiston, et al.*, 42 F.3d 691 (1st Cir. 1994).

23 *Plakas v. Drinski*, 19 F.3d 1143 (7th Cir. 1994).

24 *Salin v. Proulx*, 93 F.3d 86 (2nd Cir. 1996) (suspect grabbed officer's handgun); *Elliot v. Leavitt*, 99 F.3d 640 (4th Cir. 1996) (Handcuffed suspect pointed handgun at police); *Carter v. Buscher*, 972 F.2d 1328 (7th Cir. 1992); *Scott v. Henrich*, 39 F.2d 912 (9th Cir. 1994);

12

Federal appellate courts in these cases have consistently ruled in favor of police officers and dismissed allegations of constitutional rights violations because officers were directly challenged by suspects with life threatening activity.

In *Reese v. Anderson*[26], the Fifth Circuit Court of Appeals dismissed an action against a police officer even though the deceased suspect was later determined to have been unarmed at the time the officer shot him. The officer ordered the robbery suspect to keep his hands raised while sitting in a vehicle. The suspect ignored the officer and lowered his hands twice out of the officer's sight. During the second time, the suspect leaned over and reached toward the car floor. When the suspect popped back up, he was shot and killed. The court believed that the officer acted with a reasonable belief that he was faced with a life-threatening situation because the suspect appeared to be reaching for a weapon.

Likewise, in *Greenidge v. Ruffin*[27], the Fourth Circuit Court of Appeals ruled in favor of a police officer who shot and severely wounded a suspect who refused to place his hands in full view. Instead, the suspect reached for an object in the back seat of a vehicle that the officer

---

Menuel v. City of Atlanta, 25 F.3d 990 (11th Cir. 1994).

25   *Fraire v. City of Arlington*, 957 F.2d 1268 (5th Cir. 1992);
     Smith v. Freland, 954 F.2d 343 (6th Cir. 1992);
     Cole v. Bone, 993 F.2d 1328 (8th Cir. 1993).

26   926 F.2d 494 (5th Cir. 1991).

27   927 F.2d 789 (4th Cir. 1991). See also, *Slattery v. Rizzo*, 939 F.2d 213 (4th Cir. 1991).

thought was a shotgun. The object was later determined to be a nightstick. The court determined that the officer's use of force was reasonable.

Napier v. Town of Windham, et al.[28], presents another interesting example. Napier fired several times with a rifle into a woodpile in the front yard of his home. Neighbors called the police and two officers, the Ramsdell brothers, responded in separate cars. Richard Ramsdell arrived first, surveyed the scene by walking around the property, and approached the front door. He looked inside and saw a rifle on a table and a hand holding a handgun extending from behind a partially closed door. He claimed that he repeatedly told Napier to drop the gun but Napier ignored him. Instead, Napier walked toward him with the gun pointed at him. Richard backed up and Napier stepped into the doorway with the gun in his hand. At this point Ronald Ramsdell was standing in the driveway and later claimed that he likewise told Napier to drop the gun. The officers claimed that Napier pointed his gun at Richard and Richard retreated and fired a shot at Napier which missed. Simultaneously, Ronald fired a volley of three shots at Napier and all missed. Ronald claimed that Napier turned toward him with his gun still raised. Ronald fired three more shots and Napier was wounded.

Napier disputed the police version of events and claimed that the officers never warned him to drop his gun and denied that he ever pointed his gun at them. He

---

28   Supra, note 21.

was later convicted of criminal threatening and reckless conduct regarding Richard but acquitted of these charges regarding Ronald. He filed suit in federal court pursuant to 42 U.S.C. Sec. 1983 and claimed excessive force in violation of his Fourth Amendment rights. The District Court dismissed the lawsuit and the First Circuit Court of Appeals affirmed.

The Court of Appeals ruled that Napier's criminal conviction conclusively established that he placed Richard in fear of imminent bodily harm by means of a dangerous weapon. The court ruled that the one shot fired by Richard was objectively reasonable. Likewise, the court ruled that the first volley of shots fired by Ronald were objectively reasonable because Napier was criminally convicted for threatening his brother at the time those shots were fired.

Ronald Ramsdell's second burst of three shots was more problematic for the court because Napier claimed that the officers did not warn him to drop his weapon and he claimed he never pointed his gun at anyone. The court concluded that Ronald's decision to fire the second burst of shots was objectively reasonable, even in the absence of agreement among the parties that a warning was given. Moreover, with respect to Napier's claim that he never pointed his gun at Ronald, the court stated that Napier's self-serving claim that he did not point his gun at Ronald was not determinative. The court explained that after what had already occurred, Napier need not have specifically pointed his gun at Ronald for Ronald to believe that the danger still existed and now encompassed him.

The court appears to be saying that warning dangerous suspects is not always feasible and that an officer can be threatened with a gun, even when it is not pointed at the officer.

Dangerousness - Crimes Involving
Threatened or Actual Infliction
of Serious Bodily Harm

In *Garner* the Supreme Court limited police use of
deadly force by requiring that the suspect pose a
significant threat of death or serious bodily harm to the
officer or others. As discussed earlier in this book, this
requirement can be appropriately characterized as the
Court's dangerousness component. In explaining this
component, the *Garner* majority stated that deadly force
was appropriate if the suspect threatened the officer
with a weapon or had committed "a crime involving the
infliction or threatened infliction of serious physical
harm..."[29] The Court's language suggests that a suspect
would meet the dangerousness requirement without
threatening an officer or others with a weapon as long as
he had committed a crime involving the threatened or
actual infliction of serious bodily harm.

Ryder v. The City of Topeka[30], contains a clear explanation of *Garner's* two separate dangerousness com-
ponents. In *Ryder*, a Pizza Hut employee informed police
officers that he was supposed to be involved in a robbery
of his employer. He identified the other participants and
stated they would be armed with knives and guns. He
later told them when the robbery would occur and police
set up a stakeout. After the robbery, police moved in to

29   Supra, note 5.

30   814 F.2d 1412 (10th Cir. 1987). See also *Krueger v. Fuhr*, 991 F.2d 435 (8th Cir.
1993); *Cole v. Bone*, 973 F.2d 1328 (8th Cir. 1993); *Ayala v. Martinez*, 707
F.Supp. 75 (D. Puerto Rico 1988).

arrest the three suspects. They ran and Officer Meyer pursued Ryder. The officer fired a warning shot but Ryder continued to run. The officer fired a second shot that hit Ryder and she was seriously wounded. This shot was fired just before Ryder was about to run around a building into a darkened residential area.

The Tenth Circuit Court of Appeals affirmed a jury verdict in favor of the officer. Initially, the court observed that under the *Garner* standard: "There are two basic situations that would justify an officer's belief that a fleeing suspect poses a threat of serious physical harm: (1) where the suspect has placed the officer in a dangerous, life threatening situation; or (2) where the suspect is fleeing from the commission of an inherently violent crime. This latter situation does not require that the officer's life actually be threatened by the suspect. Rather, the officer is allowed to infer that the suspect is inherently dangerous by the violent nature of the crime."[31]

Using the *Garner* paradigm, the court rejected the officer's contention that the crime in this case was inherently violent. The court observed that the robbery was planned as an inside job in which the Pizza Hut employee (turned informer) was supposed to give away the money. The court next focused upon the issue of whether the officer had a reasonable belief that the suspect was armed. The court concluded that the officer had a reasonable belief that his life was in danger while

---

31   Id. at 1419.

he chased the suspect in the dark because she was running toward a building leading to a darkened residential area.

Forrett v. Richardson[32], is also instructive. Forrett committed a violent residential burglary in which he tied up three victims, shot one in the neck with a handgun and shot at another. He fled the scene in the victim's truck with several stolen firearms and 250 rounds of ammunition and within an hour, police officers found the truck abandoned. The stolen weapons had been removed. Minutes later, Forrett was spotted in a residential neighborhood and a foot pursuit followed. The police lost sight of Forrett and set up a perimeter around the neighborhood. They used a helicopter to warn residents because of concern that he would enter a house and take hostages. Forrett eluded capture by running across yards and streets and jumping fences. Officers confronted him in a yard bounded by a six feet high wooden fence. He turned and looked at the officers who were 20 to 30 feet away. The officers shouted at him to stop and surrender. Forrett hesitated and two officers fired seven or eight shots which missed. Forrett ran to the fence and began to climb over. Three officers fired several more shots which all missed. Forrett fell into the next yard and the officers fired through the fence. Forrett was finally hit, once in the back and once in the hip. A total of 24 rounds were fired and Forrett eventually recovered from his wounds. No weapons were found in Forrett's possession or in the vicinity of the arrest. Forrett pled guilty to the

32   112 F.3d 416 (9th Cir. 1997).

burglary and assaults and then filed an excessive force lawsuit against the individual officers who shot him, the Chief of Police and the City of Riverside, California pursuant to Title 42 U.S.C. Sec. 1983. After a jury trial, Forrett was awarded nominal and punitive damages against each defendant except the City. After the trial, the trial judge reversed the jury finding of liability and ruled as a matter of law that the officers used objectively reasonable force and that the Police Chief and the City were not liable because there was no underlying constitutional violation. Forrett appealed and the Ninth Circuit Court of Appeals affirmed.

At the outset of its opinion, the court stated that an officer can use deadly force to prevent the escape of a fleeing felon only when the officer has probable cause that the suspect poses a threat of serious harm and it is necessary to use deadly force to prevent escape.

The court next examined the meaning of when a suspect poses a threat of serious harm. The court explained that a suspect, "need not be armed or pose an immediate threat to the officers or others at the time of the shooting."[33] The court quoted language from the Supreme Court's opinion in *Tennessee v. Garner*, 471 U.S. 1 (1985) which states, "[i]f the suspect threatens the officer with a weapon or there is probable cause to believe that he has committed a crime involving the infliction or threatened infliction of serious physical harm, deadly

---

33   Id. at 420.

force may be used ..."[34] The court stated that under the *Garner* test, "it is not necessary that the suspect be armed or threaten the officer with a weapon. The court explained, *"[w]henever there is probable cause ...that the suspect has committed a crime involving the infliction or threatened infliction of serious physical harm deadly force may be used* if necessary to prevent escape, if some warning has been given where feasible."[35] The court observed that Forrett had committed a crime involving the infliction of serious harm and therefore posed a threat of serious harm to the police and others. The court also concluded that Forrett had been warned by the police before the use of deadly force and that deadly force was necessary to prevent escape.

THE NECESSITY COMPONENT

In *Garner*, the Supreme Court ruled that deadly force may only be used by law enforcement officers against dangerous suspects when necessary. Many lower federal appellate decisions following *Garner* involve fact patterns in which the dangerousness of the suspects is clear and undeniable.[36] In cases of this nature, attorneys representing plaintiffs have shifted the focus of their allegations of unconstitutional police conduct away from the clearly dangerous nature of the conduct engaged in by their clients. Instead, they have

---

34 Id.

35 Id. (emphasis added).

36 *Roy v. Inhabitants of the City of Lewiston, Et al.*, 42 F.3d 691 (1st Cir. 1994); *Schulz v. Long, Et al.*, 44 F.3d 643 (8th Cir. 1995); *Menuel v. City of Atlanta.* 25 F.3d 990 (11th Cir. 1994).

attempted to argue that the use of deadly force by the police was not necessary and that the police could have approached the problem differently. These arguments involve allegations that because the police failed to attempt different and less deadly approaches to a particular situation, they created a need to use deadly force that wasn't really necessary. Several federal appellate courts have considered and rejected lack of necessity arguments.[37]

For example in *Plakas v. Drinski*[38], Plakas resisted arrest by hitting an officer on the wrist with a fireplace poker. He ran into the woods with three officers in foot pursuit. The officers caught up to him in a clearing and tried to convince him to surrender. Plakas threatened an officer with death and charged at him with a raised fireplace poker. The officer shot and killed him and both the District Court and the Seventh Circuit Court of Appeals ruled in favor of the officer.

Plaintiff argued on appeal that the police had non-deadly alternatives available and that deadly force was not necessary. Three alternatives were suggested. First, the police could have attempted to keep a barrier (like a row of hedges) between them and Plakas. Second, they could have used a disabling spray or third, they could have used a trained dog to disarm him.

---

37   Id. See also, *Cole v. Bone*, 993 F.2d 1328 (8th Cir. 1993).

38   19 F.3d 1143 (7th Cir. 1994).

The court rejected these alternatives and stated that there is no precedent in any federal circuit that requires police use of alternatives to avoid a situation where deadly force can justifiably be used. The court explained that the Fourth Amendment does not require the use of non-deadly alternatives when deadly force is otherwise reasonable under Supreme Court precedent.

Likewise, in *Scott v. Henrich*[39], the Ninth Circuit Court of Appeals rejected claims that police officers who shot and killed an armed suspect should have taken alternative steps before confronting him. The officers responded to reports of a person firing a weapon and went to the door of the building where the suspect was believed to be located. The suspect opened the door and pointed a gun at them. The officers shot him and the lawsuit that followed was dismissed by the District Court. The Ninth Circuit affirmed and rejected lack of necessity arguments which focused on the failure of the police to develop a tactical plan, seal off escape routes, call for back-up and negotiate with the suspect rather than directly approach the front door of the suspect's location. The court ruled that as long as the police use of deadly force was reasonable, the constitution does not require them to use less intrusive alternatives.

Forrett v. Richardson[40], is also instructive. Forrett shot the victim of residential burglary in the face and escaped with several stolen firearms and ammunition.

---

39   39 F.3d 912 (9th Cir. 1994).

40   112 F.3d 416 (9th Cir. 1997).

Shortly after the burglary, officers engaged him in a foot pursuit in a residential area. He was shot twice and wounded after scaling a six-foot high fence. One shot hit him in the back and another in the hip. He survived his wounds and later sued the officers who shot him in federal court pursuant to 42 U.S.C. Sec. 1983. The trial judge ruled in favor of the police and the Ninth Circuit Court of Appeals affirmed.

On appeal, Forrett tried to convince the court that use of deadly force was not necessary because another non-deadly force alternative was available to the police. He argued that his capture was inevitable because the police had cordoned off the area and surrounded him with officers on foot and in a helicopter. The court rejected this argument and observed that the evidence did not show that an escape proof perimeter had been established at the time of the shooting. Moreover, the court stated that, "[e]ven if...capture was inevitable, it does not follow...that use of deadly force was unnecessary."[41] The court explained that the available alternative "must be reasonably likely to lead to apprehension before the suspect can cause further harm. It is not, as Forrett would have it, any alternative that might lead to apprehension in the future. The option must be reasonable in light of the community's strong interests in security and preventing further harm."[42] The court explained further that, "[t]he timing of a suspects capture, and the opportunities for violence the suspect

---

41 Id. at 420.

42 Id.

may have before capture, are therefore crucial to the reasonable necessity inquiry."[43]

Tying the above reasoning to the facts, the court noted that the suspect had tied up the residents of a private home, shot one of them and escaped with guns and ammunition. Moreover, he was fleeing through a residential area that made it "highly possible that he would... take an innocent bystander hostage."[44] The court concluded that deadly force was objectively reasonable under the circumstances and ruled that neither the Police Chief nor the City could be liable because the officers who shot Forrett did not use excessive force.

---

43 Id.

44 Id. at 421.

FEDERAL DEADLY FORCE POLICY

On October 17, 1995, Attorney General Janet Reno approved a deadly force policy for all law enforcement agencies within the U.S. Department of Justice (DOJ). This same policy has also been adopted by the Department of the Treasury, thus creating for the first time a uniform deadly force policy for all federal law enforcement agencies.[45]

The policy states that, "Law enforcement officers... may use deadly force only when necessary, that is, when the officer has a reasonable belief that the subject of such force poses an **imminent danger** of death or serious physical injury to the officer or to another person."[46] The Commentary that was issued with this policy provides an explanation for the meaning of the word "imminent."[47] The Commentary states:

" '[I]mminent' has a broader meaning than 'immediate' or 'instantaneous.' The concept of 'imminent' should be understood to be elastic, that is, involving a period of time dependent on the circumstances, rather than the fixed point of time implicit in the concept of 'immediate' or 'instantaneous.' Thus, a subject may pose an imminent danger even if he or she is not at that very moment pointing a weapon at the officer if, for example,

---

45   Supervisory Special Agent John C. Hall, (FBI), The Law Enforcement Bulletin, FBI Training on the New Federal Deadly Force Policy, April, 1996.

46   Id.

47   Id.

he or she has a weapon within reach or is running for cover carrying a weapon or running to a place where the officer has reason to believe a weapon is available."

Based upon this commentary, it is the position of the Federal Bureau of Investigation (FBI) that a suspect is **imminently** dangerous if he is running for cover while carrying a firearm even though he is not pointing the weapon at an agent at that precise moment. The FBI believes that deadly force may be used against this subject because there is no safe alternative, as long as a verbal warning is given, if feasible.[48]

By adding the imminence requirement, the Department of Justice (DOJ) is making its policy more restrictive than the constitutional standard articulated by the Supreme Court in *Garner*. As discussed previously in this article, *Garner* would permit the use of deadly force upon an escaping felon if the suspect had committed a crime involving the infliction or threatened infliction of serious bodily harm, as long as deadly force was necessary to prevent escape. The DOJ policy would not permit deadly force in that situation unless the escaping suspect presents an imminent danger to the agents or others. Under the DOJ policy, use of deadly force against an escaping felon not believed to be an imminent danger is strictly prohibited, regardless of the violent or potentially violent nature of his past crime. For example, suppose that Oklahoma City bomber Timothy McVeigh had not been arrested so quickly after the bombing. Suppose that instead, FBI Agents obtained an arrest

---

48 Id.

warrant for him and observe him a year later in a mall parking lot. At this time they have no probable cause that he is armed with a weapon. As the agents move in to make the arrest, he spots them and jumps into a nearby car. He will escape if deadly force is not used. Current DOJ policy would not permit the use of deadly force in this situation. McVeigh would be dangerous under *Garner* but not imminently dangerous as required by the DOJ policy.

THE OBJECTIVELY REASONABLE OFFICER - OFFICER SURVIVAL

It is obvious that the objectively reasonable police officer is one who has been trained by his/her department regarding the constitutional standards pertaining to the use of deadly force. Likewise, this officer must be trained and become proficient in the use of firearms as well. Responsibility for such training falls upon the police departments employing these officers.[49]

Action v. Reaction

Not so obvious, but of primary importance to an officer's survival, is the fact that an objectively reasonable officer will understand the concept of action/reaction. Several cases cited in this article contain fact patterns which involve police officers resorting to the use of deadly force as a reaction to a life threatening action directed against them by a suspect.[50] The fact that officers must often react to a life threatening action directed against them, places them at a distinct disadvantage in deadly confrontations. Physical time lag studies have established that the average human reaction time to a perceived threat is between 0.75 to 0.8 of

---

49   *City of Canton, Ohio v. Harris*, 489 U.S. 378 (1989).

50   Supra, note 30.

a second.[51] An FBI study has established that a suspect
with a gun in hand can fire two shots in 0.7 of a second.[52]
Thus, it is clear that a suspect who decides to shoot at a
police officer will be able to fire two shots before the
officer can react. This places the officer in an extremely
vulnerable position. An officer facing a person pointing
a gun directly at him, should move instantly to his right
and fire while moving. Standing still at that moment is
not a safe option.

Fleeing Armed Suspects

The concept of action/reaction makes the pursuit of
armed fleeing suspects extremely dangerous for police
officers. A fleeing suspect with gun in hand can turn and
fire at least two shots at a pursuing officer before the
officer can respond. Even more than two unanswered
shots are possible, because the pursuing officer must
stop running and steady himself before returning fire.
This further time lag would permit the suspect to fire
more unanswered shots. If the suspect's bullets are
accurate, the officer is likely to be killed or seriously
wounded without ever returning fire. The objectively
reasonable police officer will be aware of this significant
risk and should not be expected to pursue an armed

---

51   Lieutenant Michael Hillmann, (Los Angeles Police Dept.), The Tactical Edge
     magazine, Physical Lag Times and Their Impact on the Use of Deadly Force,
     p. 28, Spring 1995. Lt. Hillmann relied upon a study conducted by the U.S.
     Department of Transportation and the Federal Aviation Administration and an
     independent study conducted by the Los Angeles Police Department to support
     his conclusions.

52   See, FBI video presentation, P.I. 95-045, (show # 45), Viewpoints From The FBI
     Academy - "Deadly Force" - John C. Hall, produced by the FBI Academy,
     Quantico, Virginia.

fleeing suspect as an alternative to the use of deadly force. Pursuit in this circumstance is not a **safe alternative** to the use of deadly force.

The FBI has interpreted the new DOJ uniform policy on deadly force to permit the use of deadly force against a fleeing suspect who is running for cover with a pistol in hand. The FBI believes that this suspect poses an imminent danger to agents in the immediate vicinity and believes further that there is **no safe alternative** to the use of deadly force in this situation. As long as the suspect remains within gunshot range of the Agents, he can turn and fire before they can effectively respond (action/reaction). Attempting to pursue can only increase the risk because the suspect can hide and ambush the agents pursuing him.

The extreme danger in this context is clearly illustrated by a March, 1973 incident that involved an attempt by two FBI Agents to arrest a bank robbery suspect. The suspect had participated in an armed bank robbery the previous day. The Agents attempted to arrest him but he refused to submit and fled on foot. During the chase, he drew a handgun and eventually shot one Agent twice and killed him. The suspect shot at the other Agent and slightly wounded him also. The suspect was captured shortly thereafter but the tragic outcome of this incident serves to highlight the fact that pursuit of an armed suspect with gun in hand is **not a safe alternative** to the use of deadly force.

A recent Eleventh Circuit Court of Appeals decision, *Montoute v. Carr*,[53] is also instructive regarding the extreme danger to officers in pursuing armed fleeing suspects. In *Montoute*, two officers responded to "911" calls regarding a street fight and gunfire. Upon arrival, they heard the discharge of a shotgun. They observed Montoute approaching them, carrying a sawed-off shotgun pointed at the ground. He was ordered to drop the gun repeatedly but did not do so. He proceeded past the officers and ran. Officer Carr chased him and fired two shots. The second shot wounded Montoute in the buttocks.

Montoute sued Carr pursuant to 42 U.S.C. Sec. 1983 in federal court and the District Court refused to dismiss the suit prior to trial. The Judge explained by stating that if Montoute had his back turned and was running away, then it was questionable as to whether Carr could reasonably believe that Montoute posed a serious threat to him or others.

The Eleventh Circuit reversed and dismissed the suit. Initially, the court noted that Montoute conceded at oral argument that he posed a threat to Carr as he approached him with the shotgun at the beginning of the episode. He conceded that Carr would have been justified in shooting him at that point. Nevertheless, he argued that once he passed Carr and was running away, no reasonable officer could reasonably believe that the threat continued. The court rejected this claim and

---

53   114 F.2d 181, (11th Cir. 1997).

opined that an officer could reasonably believe that the threat continued after Montoute passed the police. The court explained that there was nothing to prevent Montoute from turning and pointing the shotgun at the pursuing officers once he passed them. The court stated that when orders to drop the weapon are ignored, police officers are not required to wait until an armed and dangerous suspect has drawn a bead on them before using deadly force. Here the court appears to be articulating the essence of the action/reaction principle.

Next, the court focused on the principle of hide and ambush. This is the other life-threatening factor in pursuit of armed suspects. The court observed that Montoute could have taken cover behind a car or the side of a building in order to surprise and shoot the officers. The court explained that if the officers had permitted Montoute to take cover or circle back behind them, he would have posed more of a danger than when he first moved toward them with the weapon at his side at the outset of the encounter.

Wounding Factors

The desired law enforcement goal in a gun battle with a dangerous suspect is to bring the life threatening confrontation to an instantaneous halt. This goal is not easily reached and is often impossible to achieve. Suspects are not likely to remain fixed in place like the paper targets on the firing range. They are likely to be moving quickly, firing rapidly, and firing from positions of partial cover. Shooting them at all in such conditions is very difficult. Even if a suspect is shot, it is likely that the deadly encounter will continue unabated. The object-ively reasonable officer knows that most gunshot wounds are not fatal, and even fatal wounds do not necessarily cause instant physiological incapacitation. A review of the shooting deaths of 56 police officers in 1990 disclosed that 16 continued to perform some deliberate function after sustaining fatal wounds. Two officers called for assistance and 15 returned fire, killing 5 suspects and wounding 5 others before dying themselves.[54]

To deprive an assailant of the ability to continue life threatening actions requires neutralization either of the central nervous system, directly by injury to the brain or upper spinal column, or indirectly through massive blood loss.[55] Barring a central nervous system or upper spinal cord hit, there is no physiological reason for an assailant to be incapacitated by even a fatal wound, until blood loss is sufficient to drop blood pressure and/or the brain is deprived of oxygen.[56] Shooting a suspect in the head or upper spinal column during a gun battle involves rare marksmanship or pure luck. Absent a direct hit in these vital areas, an instantaneous halt to the deadly confront-ation is not possible. As described above, the only other way to end the confrontation by bullet wounds involves body wounds that drop blood pressure or deprive oxygen to the brain through massive blood loss. The loss of blood

---

54   Supervisory Special Agent John C. Hall, (FBI), The Law Enforcement Bulletin, Deadly Force in defense of Life, August, 1993.

55   Id.

56   Special Agent Urey W. Patrick, (FBI), FBI Academy Firearms Training Unit, Handgun Wounding Factors and Effectiveness, P.8, July 1989.

takes time and during that time, the imminently dangerous suspect will be able to continue his mayhem upon the officers or other innocent persons. Indeed, a direct hit to the heart will not bring an instant halt to a dangerous suspect. There is sufficient oxygen within the brain to support full, voluntary action for 10 to 15 seconds after the heart has been destroyed.[57] The life ending damage that a suspect could offer in 15 seconds becomes very real when one considers that FBI Agents are required to fire 12 rounds with a magazine change from the seven yard line in 15 seconds during firearms training. Without a magazine change, even more rounds could be fired more quickly from semi- automatic pistols with high capacity magazines. Indeed, many semi-automatic pistols today are capable of firing multiple rounds with extreme rapidity. For example, the Sig Sauer P229 .40 Caliber semi-auto pistol can fire 14 rounds and can be manufactured to fire single action after the first shot is fired. Every shot fired after the first, has a trigger pull of only 4.5 pounds. Rounds in such a weapon can be fired very quickly.

Ending a dangerous confrontation by police gunfire may take seconds or minutes – depending on the location, number, and severity of the suspect's wounds – but it may suffice for the assailant to continue to carry out life-threatening actions.[58] For example, on April 11, 1986, eight FBI Agents attempted to arrest two male suspects who were responsible for a series of armored car

---

57 Id.

58 Supra, note 54.

robberies. Some of these robberies resulted in innocent victims being shot and killed. The Agents observed the suspects in a vehicle and forced the vehicle to stop. A horrendous gun battle erupted. During the firefight an Agent shot and wounded one suspect who was armed with a high powered semi-automatic rifle with a thirty round magazine. This wound was later determined to be non-survivable by medical authorities. Nevertheless, after receiving this wound, the suspect initially seriously wounded two Agents. He then aggressively approached a position where other Agents had taken cover and proceeded to shoot and kill two Agents and seriously wound another. This suspect next fired several more shots at a another Agent, narrowly missing him. Finally, the suspect was shot in the head and killed while attempting to escape in an FBI vehicle. This shooting incident resulted in the death of two Agents and the wounding of five more.[59]

This example clearly illustrates what the objectively reasonable officer should already know. A bullet simply cannot knock a man down. If it had the energy to do so, then equal energy would be applied against the shooter and he too would be knocked down. This is simple physics and has been known for hundreds of years. The amount of energy deposited in the body by a bullet is the approximate equivalent of being hit with a baseball. Tissue damage is the only physical link to incapacitation, but excluding the central nervous system, it is not

59   See, FBI video presentation, P.I. 87-320, "Firefight", produced by the FBI Academy, Quantico, Virginia, 7/28/88.

a causative factor for incapacitation within the desired time frame, i.e. instantaneously.[60]

The FBI recognizes the inherent difficulty in bringing a life-threatening incident to an instantaneous halt through the use of firearms. Accordingly, the FBI instructs its Agents that when deadly force is permissible under the new DOJ deadly force policy, attempts to shoot to cause minor injury are unrealistic and can prove dangerous to Agents and others because they are unlikely to achieve the intended purpose of bringing imminent danger to a timely halt. Instead, Agents are trained to fire at the center of their target because, of the suspect's more vulnerable body areas, this is the easiest to hit and more likely to quickly end the deadly confrontation. Proper shot placement is a hit in the center of that part of an adversary which faces the officer, regardless of anatomy or angle.[61] Training notwithstanding, a review of law enforcement shootings by the FBI clearly suggests that during a gun battle, only one or two solid torso hits on the adversary can be expected. The reason for this involves the extreme difficulty of accurately shooting a handgun under dire conditions involving sudden, unexpected and rapid movements by both the officer and the adversary. Moreover, shooting incidents often involve limited or partial target opportunities, poor lighting conditions, extreme stress and other unforeseen obstacles.[62]

---

60   Supra, note 56, p.9.

61   Supra, note 56, p.3.

62   Id.

Agents are also instructed that they may continue use of deadly force until the suspect surrenders or no longer poses an imminent danger. Police officers who fire their weapons multiple times during a life threatening confrontation are often criticized for doing so. Uninformed critics claim that such conduct amounts to excessive force. These critics fail to understand the entire discussion of wounding factors set forth above. They fail to comprehend the fact that a wounded suspect, who has not surrendered his weapon, still represents a grave danger to officers and other persons in the vicinity of the battle. Until the suspect surrenders and drops his gun, officers must be able to continue firing.

The bottom line from an officer survival standpoint is that an objectively reasonable officer must understand that wounding an armed suspect does not necessarily mean that he will die. Even if the suspect receives a non-survivable wound, it does not mean that he will die instantly. Therefore, vigilance must be maintained and force may be continued until the threat is over. Moreover, this concept works both ways. If an officer is shot, it doesn't mean that he/she will necessarily die. The officer must make a conscious decision to ignore the wound and remain in the fight. Failure to do so will allow aggressive suspects to approach the wounded officer and shoot him/her again. The officer must maintain the will to survive.

Survival Statistics

Between 1985 and 1994, 708 police officers were feloniously murdered in the line of duty. Of these, 653 were killed with firearms.[63] The objectively reasonable officer should know that 89 of those officers were killed with their own weapons.[64] This would suggest that officers should take reasonable precautionary steps to prevent this from happening. These would include utilizing holsters that bar easy access to an officer's weapon, learning proper weapon retention techniques during defensive tactics training, and waiting for proper backup when confronting potentially dangerous suspects.

Objectively reasonable officers should also know that during the above mentioned time frame, 444 of the murdered officers were not wearing body armor at the time of their demise.[65] 307 of the murdered officers received upper torso wounds and only 61 of them were wearing body armor.[66] Of the 61 wearing body armor, 31 were killed when bullets entered vest panels or arm openings. 17 received wounds above the vest area and 11 were slain when bullets penetrated the vests.[67] Although wearing a protective vest does not guarantee safety, given the availability of this life saving equipment, the consequences of failure to wear it are obvious.

---

63 Supra, note 1.

64 Id. at 4.

65 Id. at 17.

66 Id.

67 Id. at 4.

Physiological Factors

Life threatening situations are the cause of involuntary physiological reactions in the human body
that affect the performance of motor skills. Motor skills
combine cognitive processes and physical reactions to
enable a person to perform physical tasks, such as firing
a weapon. There are three types of motor skills, gross,
fine, and complex.[68]

Gross motor skills involve large muscle groups, such
as those found in the legs, arms, back, and chest. These
skills improve in deadly confrontations because of the
body's release of adrenaline and other hormones.[69]

Fine motor skills involve small muscle groups, such
as the hands and fingers. These skills require low or
nonexistent levels of stress for optimum performance
and rapidly deteriorate in life threatening situations.[70]

Complex motor skills incorporate multiple compo-
nents, often involving hand-eye coordination, timing,
balance, and tracking a moving target. Stress levels

---

68 Lt. Dean T. Olson, Douglas County Sheriff's Office, Omaha, Nebraska, FBI Law
    Enforcement Bulletin, p.4, Feb.1998. The source of this paragraph and those
    footnoted below is Lt. Olson's article.

69 Id. Lt. Olson relied on a book by B.J. Cratty, Movement Behavior and Motor
    Learning, 3d Ed. (Philadelphia, PA: Lea & Fienberger, 1973), 207-213.

70 Id. Lt. Olson relied on an article by E.C. Poulton, On Prediction in Skilled
    Movements, Psychological Bulletin, Vol.54, no.6 (1957): 467-468.

must likewise be low to reach optimum levels of performance regarding these skills.[71]

During deadly confrontations, poorly trained officers will experience escalating stress that will increase their heart rates. As the heart rate rises, fine and complex motor skills are adversely affected and will deteriorate rapidly. The rising heart rate also triggers the body's sympathetic nervous system that controls breathing and other involuntary life functions. Powerful hormones such as adrenaline and epinephrine are released into the body. These hormones further increase the heart rate and raise blood pressure. During this process, blood is directed away from the fingers and hands and extremities and toward the major muscle groups in the legs, arms, and chest. Hand dexterity and coordination drastically decline as blood vessels constrict.[72]

Eyesight is also adversely affected by increased stress. The contour of the lenses of the eyes change, making visual tracking or focusing on nearby objects, such as the front sight of a weapon, difficult or even impossible. Perpetual narrowing occurs and affects depth perception, often causing officers to fire shots low. Peripheral vision nearly vanishes as the field of vision reduces to between 12 and 18 inches.[73]

---

71   Id. Lt. Olson relied on a book by B.K. Siddle, Sharpening the Warrior's Edge: The Psychology & Science of Training (Millstadt, Il.: PPCT Research Publications, 1995), 121.

72   Id.

73   Id.

Most threats are processed through the visual sense. The significant reduction in visual input severely restricts the brain's ability to receive and process vital information. Research has shown that when peripheral vision decreases 70 percent, it takes a person up to 440 percent more time to react.[74]

It is obvious that a loss of fine and complex motor skills and vision place police officers at great risk during deadly confrontations. Moreover, if an officer's heart rate remains unchecked, a survival stress response called "hypervigilance" occurs. This will cause an officer to freeze in place or act irrationally in a panic or near panic condition.[75]

The key to managing survival stress is controlling the heart rate. The optimal heart rate for combat performance is between 115 and 145 beats per minute (BPM). Cognitive skills begin to deteriorate at rates above 155 BPM. Perceptual narrowing, and hypervigilance begin at 175 BPM. Officers experience full-blown hypervigilance at rates between 200 and 225 BPM.[76] Not uncommonly, officers experiencing hypervigilance might repeatedly pull the trigger on an empty weapon, misidentify innocuous items as weapons, or not see or hear innocent bystanders in the line of fire.[77]

---

74   Id. at 4-5.

75   Id. at 5. For Lt. Olson's source, see note 71, p.85.

76   Id.

77   Id.

As mentioned above, controlling the heart rate is essential to the successful outcome of a deadly confrontation. One method to assist officers in controlling their heart rate involves placing them in realistic simulated deadly force training situations involving live or on screen adversaries. The FBI uses both an interactive video system known as the Firearms Training System (FATS) and live paintball exercises to place agents in realistic potential deadly force situations. This enables the agents to experience the physiological factors described above in a training setting where they can learn to control their breathing and keep their heart rates below the danger zone. The time for an officer to learn about the potential for spiraling heart rates is not during a real life and death confrontation with a person who is trying to kill him. Realistic deadly force training will allow the officer to experience the potential for accelerating heart rates and make a conscious effort to control breathing. Through repeated training situations, officers will learn to control breathing and observe better success in the outcome of the training as breathing is successfully managed. Officers will also learn first hand the concept of action/reaction, the need to make use of available cover, the need for rapid but accurate shooting, and the difficulty in hitting moving targets who are also firing weapons in their direction. They will also be confronted with some situations in which the use of deadly force would be inappropriate because its use would violate the constitution and/or deadly force policy. It is the duty of every law enforcement agency to regularly expose their officers to realistic simulated deadly force training. The well-trained, objectively reasonable officer will know what to expect before ever entering a deadly confrontation. This will dramatically increase his/her chances for survival.

INDEX